MY BUG
LOG BOOK

THIS BOOK BELONGS TO:

_____

_____

_____

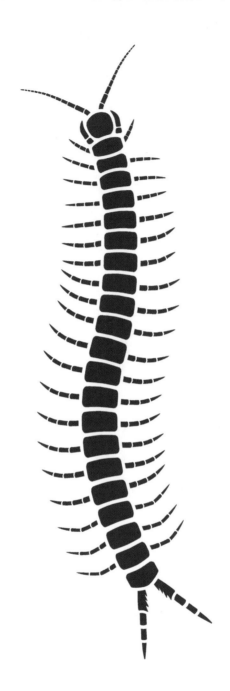

Copyright © 2021 by Rene V. Downs

BUG IDENTIFICATION LOG

DATE:	TIME:	SEASON:

LOCATION:

BUG NAME:

BUG COLORS:

NUMBER OF LEGS:	DOES IT HAVE WINGS: ☐ YES ☐ NO ☐ NOT SURE

BUG DESCRIPTION:

DOES IT MAKE ANY SOUNDS? ☐ YES ☐ NO	WAS IT ALONE OR IN A GROUP? ☐ ALONE ☐ GROUP

BUG'S ACTIONS:

PHOTO/DRAWING

NOTES:

BUG IDENTIFICATION LOG

DATE:	TIME:	SEASON:

LOCATION:

BUG NAME:

BUG COLORS:

NUMBER OF LEGS:	DOES IT HAVE WINGS: ☐ YES ☐ NO ☐ NOT SURE

BUG DESCRIPTION:

DOES IT MAKE ANY SOUNDS? ☐ YES ☐ NO	WAS IT ALONE OR IN A GROUP? ☐ ALONE ☐ GROUP

BUG'S ACTIONS:

PHOTO/DRAWING

NOTES:

BUG IDENTIFICATION LOG

DATE:	TIME:	SEASON:

LOCATION:

BUG NAME:

BUG COLORS:

NUMBER OF LEGS:	DOES IT HAVE WINGS: ☐ YES ☐ NO ☐ NOT SURE

BUG DESCRIPTION:

DOES IT MAKE ANY SOUNDS? ☐ YES ☐ NO	WAS IT ALONE OR IN A GROUP? ☐ ALONE ☐ GROUP

BUG'S ACTIONS:

PHOTO/DRAWING

NOTES:

BUG IDENTIFICATION LOG

DATE:	TIME:	SEASON:

LOCATION:

BUG NAME:

BUG COLORS:

NUMBER OF LEGS:	DOES IT HAVE WINGS: ☐ YES ☐ NO ☐ NOT SURE

BUG DESCRIPTION:

DOES IT MAKE ANY SOUNDS? ☐ YES ☐ NO	WAS IT ALONE OR IN A GROUP? ☐ ALONE ☐ GROUP

BUG'S ACTIONS:

PHOTO/DRAWING

NOTES:

BUG IDENTIFICATION LOG

DATE:	TIME:	SEASON:

LOCATION:

BUG NAME:

BUG COLORS:

NUMBER OF LEGS:	DOES IT HAVE WINGS: ☐ YES ☐ NO ☐ NOT SURE

BUG DESCRIPTION:

DOES IT MAKE ANY SOUNDS? ☐ YES ☐ NO	WAS IT ALONE OR IN A GROUP? ☐ ALONE ☐ GROUP

BUG'S ACTIONS:

PHOTO/DRAWING

NOTES:

BUG IDENTIFICATION LOG

DATE:	TIME:	SEASON:

LOCATION:

BUG NAME:

BUG COLORS:

NUMBER OF LEGS:	DOES IT HAVE WINGS: ☐ YES ☐ NO ☐ NOT SURE

BUG DESCRIPTION:

DOES IT MAKE ANY SOUNDS? ☐ YES ☐ NO	WAS IT ALONE OR IN A GROUP? ☐ ALONE ☐ GROUP

BUG'S ACTIONS:

PHOTO/DRAWING

NOTES:

BUG IDENTIFICATION LOG

DATE: | TIME: | SEASON:

LOCATION:

BUG NAME:

BUG COLORS:

NUMBER OF LEGS: | DOES IT HAVE WINGS: ☐ YES ☐ NO ☐ NOT SURE

BUG DESCRIPTION:

DOES IT MAKE ANY SOUNDS? ☐ YES ☐ NO | WAS IT ALONE OR IN A GROUP? ☐ ALONE ☐ GROUP

BUG'S ACTIONS:

PHOTO/DRAWING

NOTES:

BUG IDENTIFICATION LOG

DATE:	TIME:	SEASON:

LOCATION:

BUG NAME:

BUG COLORS:

NUMBER OF LEGS:	DOES IT HAVE WINGS: ☐ YES ☐ NO ☐ NOT SURE

BUG DESCRIPTION:

DOES IT MAKE ANY SOUNDS? ☐ YES ☐ NO	WAS IT ALONE OR IN A GROUP? ☐ ALONE ☐ GROUP

BUG'S ACTIONS:

PHOTO/DRAWING

NOTES:

BUG IDENTIFICATION LOG

DATE:	TIME:	SEASON:

LOCATION:

BUG NAME:

BUG COLORS:

NUMBER OF LEGS:	DOES IT HAVE WINGS: ☐ YES ☐ NO ☐ NOT SURE

BUG DESCRIPTION:

DOES IT MAKE ANY SOUNDS? ☐ YES ☐ NO | WAS IT ALONE OR IN A GROUP? ☐ ALONE ☐ GROUP

BUG'S ACTIONS:

PHOTO/DRAWING

NOTES:

BUG IDENTIFICATION LOG

DATE:	TIME:	SEASON:

LOCATION:

BUG NAME:

BUG COLORS:

NUMBER OF LEGS:	DOES IT HAVE WINGS: ☐ YES ☐ NO ☐ NOT SURE

BUG DESCRIPTION:

DOES IT MAKE ANY SOUNDS? ☐ YES ☐ NO	WAS IT ALONE OR IN A GROUP? ☐ ALONE ☐ GROUP

BUG'S ACTIONS:

PHOTO/DRAWING

NOTES:

BUG IDENTIFICATION LOG

DATE:	TIME:	SEASON:

LOCATION:

BUG NAME:

BUG COLORS:

NUMBER OF LEGS:	DOES IT HAVE WINGS: ☐ YES ☐ NO ☐ NOT SURE

BUG DESCRIPTION:

DOES IT MAKE ANY SOUNDS? ☐ YES ☐ NO	WAS IT ALONE OR IN A GROUP? ☐ ALONE ☐ GROUP

BUG'S ACTIONS:

PHOTO/DRAWING

NOTES:

BUG IDENTIFICATION LOG

DATE:	TIME:	SEASON:

LOCATION:

BUG NAME:

BUG COLORS:

NUMBER OF LEGS:	DOES IT HAVE WINGS: ☐ YES ☐ NO ☐ NOT SURE

BUG DESCRIPTION:

DOES IT MAKE ANY SOUNDS? ☐ YES ☐ NO | WAS IT ALONE OR IN A GROUP? ☐ ALONE ☐ GROUP

BUG'S ACTIONS:

PHOTO/DRAWING

NOTES:

BUG IDENTIFICATION LOG

DATE:	TIME:	SEASON:

LOCATION:

BUG NAME:

BUG COLORS:

NUMBER OF LEGS:	DOES IT HAVE WINGS: ☐ YES ☐ NO ☐ NOT SURE

BUG DESCRIPTION:

DOES IT MAKE ANY SOUNDS? ☐ YES ☐ NO	WAS IT ALONE OR IN A GROUP? ☐ ALONE ☐ GROUP

BUG'S ACTIONS:

PHOTO/DRAWING

NOTES:

BUG IDENTIFICATION LOG

DATE:	TIME:	SEASON:

LOCATION:

BUG NAME:

BUG COLORS:

NUMBER OF LEGS:	DOES IT HAVE WINGS: ☐ YES ☐ NO ☐ NOT SURE

BUG DESCRIPTION:

DOES IT MAKE ANY SOUNDS? ☐ YES ☐ NO	WAS IT ALONE OR IN A GROUP? ☐ ALONE ☐ GROUP

BUG'S ACTIONS:

PHOTO/DRAWING

NOTES:

BUG IDENTIFICATION LOG

DATE:	TIME:	SEASON:

LOCATION:

BUG NAME:

BUG COLORS:

NUMBER OF LEGS:	DOES IT HAVE WINGS: ☐ YES ☐ NO ☐ NOT SURE

BUG DESCRIPTION:

DOES IT MAKE ANY SOUNDS? ☐ YES ☐ NO	WAS IT ALONE OR IN A GROUP? ☐ ALONE ☐ GROUP

BUG'S ACTIONS:

PHOTO/DRAWING

NOTES:

BUG IDENTIFICATION LOG

DATE:	TIME:	SEASON:

LOCATION:

BUG NAME:

BUG COLORS:

NUMBER OF LEGS:	DOES IT HAVE WINGS: ☐ YES ☐ NO ☐ NOT SURE

BUG DESCRIPTION:

DOES IT MAKE ANY SOUNDS? ☐ YES ☐ NO	WAS IT ALONE OR IN A GROUP? ☐ ALONE ☐ GROUP

BUG'S ACTIONS:

PHOTO/DRAWING

NOTES:

BUG IDENTIFICATION LOG

DATE: | TIME: | SEASON:

LOCATION:

BUG NAME:

BUG COLORS:

NUMBER OF LEGS: | DOES IT HAVE WINGS: ☐ YES ☐ NO ☐ NOT SURE

BUG DESCRIPTION:

DOES IT MAKE ANY SOUNDS? ☐ YES ☐ NO | WAS IT ALONE OR IN A GROUP? ☐ ALONE ☐ GROUP

BUG'S ACTIONS:

PHOTO/DRAWING

NOTES:

BUG IDENTIFICATION LOG

DATE:	TIME:	SEASON:

LOCATION:

BUG NAME:

BUG COLORS:

NUMBER OF LEGS:	DOES IT HAVE WINGS: ☐ YES ☐ NO ☐ NOT SURE

BUG DESCRIPTION:

DOES IT MAKE ANY SOUNDS? ☐ YES ☐ NO	WAS IT ALONE OR IN A GROUP? ☐ ALONE ☐ GROUP

BUG'S ACTIONS:

PHOTO/DRAWING

NOTES:

BUG IDENTIFICATION LOG

DATE:	TIME:	SEASON:

LOCATION:

BUG NAME:

BUG COLORS:

NUMBER OF LEGS:	DOES IT HAVE WINGS: ☐ YES ☐ NO ☐ NOT SURE

BUG DESCRIPTION:

DOES IT MAKE ANY SOUNDS? ☐ YES ☐ NO	WAS IT ALONE OR IN A GROUP? ☐ ALONE ☐ GROUP

BUG'S ACTIONS:

PHOTO/DRAWING

NOTES:

BUG IDENTIFICATION LOG

DATE:	TIME:	SEASON:

LOCATION:

BUG NAME:

BUG COLORS:

NUMBER OF LEGS:	DOES IT HAVE WINGS: ☐ YES ☐ NO ☐ NOT SURE

BUG DESCRIPTION:

DOES IT MAKE ANY SOUNDS? ☐ YES ☐ NO	WAS IT ALONE OR IN A GROUP? ☐ ALONE ☐ GROUP

BUG'S ACTIONS:

PHOTO/DRAWING

NOTES:

BUG IDENTIFICATION LOG

DATE:	TIME:	SEASON:

LOCATION:

BUG NAME:

BUG COLORS:

NUMBER OF LEGS:	DOES IT HAVE WINGS: ☐ YES ☐ NO ☐ NOT SURE

BUG DESCRIPTION:

DOES IT MAKE ANY SOUNDS? ☐ YES ☐ NO	WAS IT ALONE OR IN A GROUP? ☐ ALONE ☐ GROUP

BUG'S ACTIONS:

PHOTO/DRAWING

NOTES:

BUG IDENTIFICATION LOG

DATE:	TIME:	SEASON:

LOCATION:

BUG NAME:

BUG COLORS:

NUMBER OF LEGS:	DOES IT HAVE WINGS: ☐ YES ☐ NO ☐ NOT SURE

BUG DESCRIPTION:

DOES IT MAKE ANY SOUNDS? ☐ YES ☐ NO	WAS IT ALONE OR IN A GROUP? ☐ ALONE ☐ GROUP

BUG'S ACTIONS:

PHOTO/DRAWING

NOTES:

BUG IDENTIFICATION LOG

DATE:	TIME:	SEASON:

LOCATION:

BUG NAME:

BUG COLORS:

NUMBER OF LEGS:	DOES IT HAVE WINGS: ☐ YES ☐ NO ☐ NOT SURE

BUG DESCRIPTION:

DOES IT MAKE ANY SOUNDS? ☐ YES ☐ NO	WAS IT ALONE OR IN A GROUP? ☐ ALONE ☐ GROUP

BUG'S ACTIONS:

PHOTO/DRAWING

NOTES:

BUG IDENTIFICATION LOG

DATE:	TIME:	SEASON:

LOCATION:

BUG NAME:

BUG COLORS:

NUMBER OF LEGS:	DOES IT HAVE WINGS: ☐ YES ☐ NO ☐ NOT SURE

BUG DESCRIPTION:

DOES IT MAKE ANY SOUNDS? ☐ YES ☐ NO	WAS IT ALONE OR IN A GROUP? ☐ ALONE ☐ GROUP

BUG'S ACTIONS:

PHOTO/DRAWING

NOTES:

BUG IDENTIFICATION LOG

DATE:	TIME:	SEASON:

LOCATION:

BUG NAME:

BUG COLORS:

NUMBER OF LEGS:	DOES IT HAVE WINGS: ☐ YES ☐ NO ☐ NOT SURE

BUG DESCRIPTION:

DOES IT MAKE ANY SOUNDS? ☐ YES ☐ NO	WAS IT ALONE OR IN A GROUP? ☐ ALONE ☐ GROUP

BUG'S ACTIONS:

PHOTO/DRAWING

NOTES:

BUG IDENTIFICATION LOG

DATE:	TIME:	SEASON:

LOCATION:

BUG NAME:

BUG COLORS:

NUMBER OF LEGS:	DOES IT HAVE WINGS: ☐ YES ☐ NO ☐ NOT SURE

BUG DESCRIPTION:

DOES IT MAKE ANY SOUNDS? ☐ YES ☐ NO	WAS IT ALONE OR IN A GROUP? ☐ ALONE ☐ GROUP

BUG'S ACTIONS:

PHOTO/DRAWING

NOTES:

BUG IDENTIFICATION LOG

DATE: | TIME: | SEASON:

LOCATION:

BUG NAME:

BUG COLORS:

NUMBER OF LEGS: | DOES IT HAVE WINGS: ☐ YES ☐ NO ☐ NOT SURE

BUG DESCRIPTION:

DOES IT MAKE ANY SOUNDS? ☐ YES ☐ NO | WAS IT ALONE OR IN A GROUP? ☐ ALONE ☐ GROUP

BUG'S ACTIONS:

PHOTO/DRAWING

NOTES:

BUG IDENTIFICATION LOG

DATE: | TIME: | SEASON:

LOCATION:

BUG NAME:

BUG COLORS:

NUMBER OF LEGS: | DOES IT HAVE WINGS: ☐ YES ☐ NO ☐ NOT SURE

BUG DESCRIPTION:

DOES IT MAKE ANY SOUNDS? ☐ YES ☐ NO | WAS IT ALONE OR IN A GROUP? ☐ ALONE ☐ GROUP

BUG'S ACTIONS:

PHOTO/DRAWING

NOTES:

BUG IDENTIFICATION LOG

DATE: | TIME: | SEASON:

LOCATION:

BUG NAME:

BUG COLORS:

NUMBER OF LEGS: | DOES IT HAVE WINGS: ☐ YES ☐ NO ☐ NOT SURE

BUG DESCRIPTION:

DOES IT MAKE ANY SOUNDS? ☐ YES ☐ NO | WAS IT ALONE OR IN A GROUP? ☐ ALONE ☐ GROUP

BUG'S ACTIONS:

PHOTO/DRAWING

NOTES:

BUG IDENTIFICATION LOG

DATE: | TIME: | SEASON:

LOCATION:

BUG NAME:

BUG COLORS:

NUMBER OF LEGS: | DOES IT HAVE WINGS: ☐ YES ☐ NO ☐ NOT SURE

BUG DESCRIPTION:

DOES IT MAKE ANY SOUNDS? ☐ YES ☐ NO | WAS IT ALONE OR IN A GROUP? ☐ ALONE ☐ GROUP

BUG'S ACTIONS:

PHOTO/DRAWING

NOTES:

BUG IDENTIFICATION LOG

DATE:	TIME:	SEASON:

LOCATION:

BUG NAME:

BUG COLORS:

NUMBER OF LEGS:	DOES IT HAVE WINGS: ☐ YES ☐ NO ☐ NOT SURE

BUG DESCRIPTION:

DOES IT MAKE ANY SOUNDS? ☐ YES ☐ NO	WAS IT ALONE OR IN A GROUP? ☐ ALONE ☐ GROUP

BUG'S ACTIONS:

PHOTO/DRAWING

NOTES:

BUG IDENTIFICATION LOG

DATE: | TIME: | SEASON:

LOCATION:

BUG NAME:

BUG COLORS:

NUMBER OF LEGS: | DOES IT HAVE WINGS: ☐ YES ☐ NO ☐ NOT SURE

BUG DESCRIPTION:

DOES IT MAKE ANY SOUNDS? ☐ YES ☐ NO | WAS IT ALONE OR IN A GROUP? ☐ ALONE ☐ GROUP

BUG'S ACTIONS:

PHOTO/DRAWING

NOTES:

BUG IDENTIFICATION LOG

DATE:	TIME:	SEASON:

LOCATION:

BUG NAME:

BUG COLORS:

NUMBER OF LEGS:	DOES IT HAVE WINGS: ☐ YES ☐ NO ☐ NOT SURE

BUG DESCRIPTION:

DOES IT MAKE ANY SOUNDS? ☐ YES ☐ NO	WAS IT ALONE OR IN A GROUP? ☐ ALONE ☐ GROUP

BUG'S ACTIONS:

PHOTO/DRAWING

NOTES:

BUG IDENTIFICATION LOG

DATE:	TIME:	SEASON:

LOCATION:

BUG NAME:

BUG COLORS:

NUMBER OF LEGS:	DOES IT HAVE WINGS: ☐ YES ☐ NO ☐ NOT SURE

BUG DESCRIPTION:

DOES IT MAKE ANY SOUNDS? ☐ YES ☐ NO	WAS IT ALONE OR IN A GROUP? ☐ ALONE ☐ GROUP

BUG'S ACTIONS:

PHOTO/DRAWING

NOTES:

BUG IDENTIFICATION LOG

DATE:	TIME:	SEASON:

LOCATION:

BUG NAME:

BUG COLORS:

NUMBER OF LEGS:	DOES IT HAVE WINGS: ☐ YES ☐ NO ☐ NOT SURE

BUG DESCRIPTION:

DOES IT MAKE ANY SOUNDS? ☐ YES ☐ NO	WAS IT ALONE OR IN A GROUP? ☐ ALONE ☐ GROUP

BUG'S ACTIONS:

PHOTO/DRAWING

NOTES:

BUG IDENTIFICATION LOG

DATE:	TIME:	SEASON:

LOCATION:

BUG NAME:

BUG COLORS:

NUMBER OF LEGS:	DOES IT HAVE WINGS: ☐ YES ☐ NO ☐ NOT SURE

BUG DESCRIPTION:

DOES IT MAKE ANY SOUNDS? ☐ YES ☐ NO	WAS IT ALONE OR IN A GROUP? ☐ ALONE ☐ GROUP

BUG'S ACTIONS:

PHOTO/DRAWING

NOTES:

BUG IDENTIFICATION LOG

DATE:	TIME:	SEASON:

LOCATION:

BUG NAME:

BUG COLORS:

NUMBER OF LEGS:	DOES IT HAVE WINGS:	☐ YES	☐ NO	☐ NOT SURE

BUG DESCRIPTION:

DOES IT MAKE ANY SOUNDS? ☐ YES ☐ NO	WAS IT ALONE OR IN A GROUP? ☐ ALONE ☐ GROUP

BUG'S ACTIONS:

PHOTO/DRAWING

NOTES:

BUG IDENTIFICATION LOG

DATE:	TIME:	SEASON:

LOCATION:

BUG NAME:

BUG COLORS:

NUMBER OF LEGS:	DOES IT HAVE WINGS: ☐ YES ☐ NO ☐ NOT SURE

BUG DESCRIPTION:

DOES IT MAKE ANY SOUNDS? ☐ YES ☐ NO	WAS IT ALONE OR IN A GROUP? ☐ ALONE ☐ GROUP

BUG'S ACTIONS:

PHOTO/DRAWING

NOTES:

BUG IDENTIFICATION LOG

DATE:	TIME:	SEASON:

LOCATION:

BUG NAME:

BUG COLORS:

NUMBER OF LEGS:	DOES IT HAVE WINGS: ☐ YES ☐ NO ☐ NOT SURE

BUG DESCRIPTION:

DOES IT MAKE ANY SOUNDS? ☐ YES ☐ NO	WAS IT ALONE OR IN A GROUP? ☐ ALONE ☐ GROUP

BUG'S ACTIONS:

PHOTO/DRAWING

NOTES:

BUG IDENTIFICATION LOG

DATE:	TIME:	SEASON:

LOCATION:

BUG NAME:

BUG COLORS:

NUMBER OF LEGS:	DOES IT HAVE WINGS: ☐ YES ☐ NO ☐ NOT SURE

BUG DESCRIPTION:

DOES IT MAKE ANY SOUNDS? ☐ YES ☐ NO	WAS IT ALONE OR IN A GROUP? ☐ ALONE ☐ GROUP

BUG'S ACTIONS:

PHOTO/DRAWING

NOTES:

BUG IDENTIFICATION LOG

DATE: | TIME: | SEASON:

LOCATION:

BUG NAME:

BUG COLORS:

NUMBER OF LEGS: | DOES IT HAVE WINGS: ☐ YES ☐ NO ☐ NOT SURE

BUG DESCRIPTION:

DOES IT MAKE ANY SOUNDS? ☐ YES ☐ NO | WAS IT ALONE OR IN A GROUP? ☐ ALONE ☐ GROUP

BUG'S ACTIONS:

PHOTO/DRAWING

NOTES:

BUG IDENTIFICATION LOG

DATE:	TIME:	SEASON:

LOCATION:

BUG NAME:

BUG COLORS:

NUMBER OF LEGS:	DOES IT HAVE WINGS: ☐ YES ☐ NO ☐ NOT SURE

BUG DESCRIPTION:

DOES IT MAKE ANY SOUNDS? ☐ YES ☐ NO	WAS IT ALONE OR IN A GROUP? ☐ ALONE ☐ GROUP

BUG'S ACTIONS:

PHOTO/DRAWING

NOTES:

BUG IDENTIFICATION LOG

DATE:	TIME:	SEASON:

LOCATION:

BUG NAME:

BUG COLORS:

NUMBER OF LEGS:	DOES IT HAVE WINGS: ☐ YES ☐ NO ☐ NOT SURE

BUG DESCRIPTION:

DOES IT MAKE ANY SOUNDS? ☐ YES ☐ NO	WAS IT ALONE OR IN A GROUP? ☐ ALONE ☐ GROUP

BUG'S ACTIONS:

PHOTO/DRAWING

NOTES:

BUG IDENTIFICATION LOG

DATE: | TIME: | SEASON:

LOCATION:

BUG NAME:

BUG COLORS:

NUMBER OF LEGS: | DOES IT HAVE WINGS: ☐ YES ☐ NO ☐ NOT SURE

BUG DESCRIPTION:

DOES IT MAKE ANY SOUNDS? ☐ YES ☐ NO | WAS IT ALONE OR IN A GROUP? ☐ ALONE ☐ GROUP

BUG'S ACTIONS:

PHOTO/DRAWING

NOTES:

BUG IDENTIFICATION LOG

DATE:	TIME:	SEASON:

LOCATION:

BUG NAME:

BUG COLORS:

NUMBER OF LEGS:	DOES IT HAVE WINGS: ☐ YES ☐ NO ☐ NOT SURE

BUG DESCRIPTION:

DOES IT MAKE ANY SOUNDS? ☐ YES ☐ NO	WAS IT ALONE OR IN A GROUP? ☐ ALONE ☐ GROUP

BUG'S ACTIONS:

PHOTO/DRAWING

NOTES:

BUG IDENTIFICATION LOG

DATE: | TIME: | SEASON:

LOCATION:

BUG NAME:

BUG COLORS:

NUMBER OF LEGS: | DOES IT HAVE WINGS: ☐ YES ☐ NO ☐ NOT SURE

BUG DESCRIPTION:

DOES IT MAKE ANY SOUNDS? ☐ YES ☐ NO | WAS IT ALONE OR IN A GROUP? ☐ ALONE ☐ GROUP

BUG'S ACTIONS:

PHOTO/DRAWING

NOTES:

BUG IDENTIFICATION LOG

DATE:	TIME:	SEASON:

LOCATION:

BUG NAME:

BUG COLORS:

NUMBER OF LEGS:	DOES IT HAVE WINGS: ☐ YES ☐ NO ☐ NOT SURE

BUG DESCRIPTION:

DOES IT MAKE ANY SOUNDS? ☐ YES ☐ NO	WAS IT ALONE OR IN A GROUP? ☐ ALONE ☐ GROUP

BUG'S ACTIONS:

PHOTO/DRAWING

NOTES:

BUG IDENTIFICATION LOG

DATE:	TIME:	SEASON:

LOCATION:

BUG NAME:

BUG COLORS:

NUMBER OF LEGS:	DOES IT HAVE WINGS: ☐ YES ☐ NO ☐ NOT SURE

BUG DESCRIPTION:

DOES IT MAKE ANY SOUNDS? ☐ YES ☐ NO	WAS IT ALONE OR IN A GROUP? ☐ ALONE ☐ GROUP

BUG'S ACTIONS:

PHOTO/DRAWING

NOTES:

BUG IDENTIFICATION LOG

DATE:	TIME:	SEASON:

LOCATION:

BUG NAME:

BUG COLORS:

NUMBER OF LEGS:	DOES IT HAVE WINGS: ☐ YES ☐ NO ☐ NOT SURE

BUG DESCRIPTION:

DOES IT MAKE ANY SOUNDS? ☐ YES ☐ NO	WAS IT ALONE OR IN A GROUP? ☐ ALONE ☐ GROUP

BUG'S ACTIONS:

PHOTO/DRAWING

NOTES:

BUG IDENTIFICATION LOG

DATE:	TIME:	SEASON:

LOCATION:

BUG NAME:

BUG COLORS:

NUMBER OF LEGS:	DOES IT HAVE WINGS: ☐ YES ☐ NO ☐ NOT SURE

BUG DESCRIPTION:

DOES IT MAKE ANY SOUNDS? ☐ YES ☐ NO | WAS IT ALONE OR IN A GROUP? ☐ ALONE ☐ GROUP

BUG'S ACTIONS:

PHOTO/DRAWING

NOTES:

BUG IDENTIFICATION LOG

DATE:	TIME:	SEASON:

LOCATION:

BUG NAME:

BUG COLORS:

NUMBER OF LEGS:	DOES IT HAVE WINGS: ☐ YES ☐ NO ☐ NOT SURE

BUG DESCRIPTION:

DOES IT MAKE ANY SOUNDS? ☐ YES ☐ NO	WAS IT ALONE OR IN A GROUP? ☐ ALONE ☐ GROUP

BUG'S ACTIONS:

PHOTO/DRAWING

NOTES:

BUG IDENTIFICATION LOG

DATE:	TIME:	SEASON:

LOCATION:

BUG NAME:

BUG COLORS:

NUMBER OF LEGS:	DOES IT HAVE WINGS: ☐ YES ☐ NO ☐ NOT SURE

BUG DESCRIPTION:

DOES IT MAKE ANY SOUNDS? ☐ YES ☐ NO	WAS IT ALONE OR IN A GROUP? ☐ ALONE ☐ GROUP

BUG'S ACTIONS:

PHOTO/DRAWING

NOTES:

BUG IDENTIFICATION LOG

DATE:	TIME:	SEASON:

LOCATION:

BUG NAME:

BUG COLORS:

NUMBER OF LEGS:	DOES IT HAVE WINGS: ☐ YES ☐ NO ☐ NOT SURE

BUG DESCRIPTION:

DOES IT MAKE ANY SOUNDS? ☐ YES ☐ NO	WAS IT ALONE OR IN A GROUP? ☐ ALONE ☐ GROUP

BUG'S ACTIONS:

PHOTO/DRAWING

NOTES:

BUG IDENTIFICATION LOG

DATE:	TIME:	SEASON:

LOCATION:

BUG NAME:

BUG COLORS:

NUMBER OF LEGS:	DOES IT HAVE WINGS: ☐ YES ☐ NO ☐ NOT SURE

BUG DESCRIPTION:

DOES IT MAKE ANY SOUNDS? ☐ YES ☐ NO	WAS IT ALONE OR IN A GROUP? ☐ ALONE ☐ GROUP

BUG'S ACTIONS:

PHOTO/DRAWING

NOTES:

BUG IDENTIFICATION LOG

DATE:	TIME:	SEASON:

LOCATION:

BUG NAME:

BUG COLORS:

NUMBER OF LEGS:	DOES IT HAVE WINGS: ☐ YES ☐ NO ☐ NOT SURE

BUG DESCRIPTION:

DOES IT MAKE ANY SOUNDS? ☐ YES ☐ NO	WAS IT ALONE OR IN A GROUP? ☐ ALONE ☐ GROUP

BUG'S ACTIONS:

PHOTO/DRAWING

NOTES:

BUG IDENTIFICATION LOG

DATE:	TIME:	SEASON:

LOCATION:

BUG NAME:

BUG COLORS:

NUMBER OF LEGS:	DOES IT HAVE WINGS: ☐ YES ☐ NO ☐ NOT SURE

BUG DESCRIPTION:

DOES IT MAKE ANY SOUNDS? ☐ YES ☐ NO	WAS IT ALONE OR IN A GROUP? ☐ ALONE ☐ GROUP

BUG'S ACTIONS:

PHOTO/DRAWING

NOTES:

BUG IDENTIFICATION LOG

DATE:	TIME:	SEASON:

LOCATION:

BUG NAME:

BUG COLORS:

NUMBER OF LEGS:	DOES IT HAVE WINGS: ☐ YES ☐ NO ☐ NOT SURE

BUG DESCRIPTION:

DOES IT MAKE ANY SOUNDS? ☐ YES ☐ NO	WAS IT ALONE OR IN A GROUP? ☐ ALONE ☐ GROUP

BUG'S ACTIONS:

PHOTO/DRAWING

NOTES:

BUG IDENTIFICATION LOG

DATE:	TIME:	SEASON:

LOCATION:

BUG NAME:

BUG COLORS:

NUMBER OF LEGS:	DOES IT HAVE WINGS: ☐ YES ☐ NO ☐ NOT SURE

BUG DESCRIPTION:

DOES IT MAKE ANY SOUNDS? ☐ YES ☐ NO	WAS IT ALONE OR IN A GROUP? ☐ ALONE ☐ GROUP

BUG'S ACTIONS:

PHOTO/DRAWING

NOTES:

BUG IDENTIFICATION LOG

DATE: | TIME: | SEASON:

LOCATION:

BUG NAME:

BUG COLORS:

NUMBER OF LEGS: | DOES IT HAVE WINGS: ☐ YES ☐ NO ☐ NOT SURE

BUG DESCRIPTION:

DOES IT MAKE ANY SOUNDS? ☐ YES ☐ NO | WAS IT ALONE OR IN A GROUP? ☐ ALONE ☐ GROUP

BUG'S ACTIONS:

PHOTO/DRAWING

NOTES:

BUG IDENTIFICATION LOG

DATE:	TIME:	SEASON:

LOCATION:

BUG NAME:

BUG COLORS:

NUMBER OF LEGS:	DOES IT HAVE WINGS: ☐ YES ☐ NO ☐ NOT SURE

BUG DESCRIPTION:

DOES IT MAKE ANY SOUNDS? ☐ YES ☐ NO	WAS IT ALONE OR IN A GROUP? ☐ ALONE ☐ GROUP

BUG'S ACTIONS:

PHOTO/DRAWING

NOTES:

BUG IDENTIFICATION LOG

DATE:	TIME:	SEASON:

LOCATION:

BUG NAME:

BUG COLORS:

NUMBER OF LEGS:	DOES IT HAVE WINGS: ☐ YES ☐ NO ☐ NOT SURE

BUG DESCRIPTION:

DOES IT MAKE ANY SOUNDS? ☐ YES ☐ NO	WAS IT ALONE OR IN A GROUP? ☐ ALONE ☐ GROUP

BUG'S ACTIONS:

PHOTO/DRAWING

NOTES:

BUG IDENTIFICATION LOG

DATE:	TIME:	SEASON:

LOCATION:

BUG NAME:

BUG COLORS:

NUMBER OF LEGS:	DOES IT HAVE WINGS: ☐ YES ☐ NO ☐ NOT SURE

BUG DESCRIPTION:

DOES IT MAKE ANY SOUNDS? ☐ YES ☐ NO	WAS IT ALONE OR IN A GROUP? ☐ ALONE ☐ GROUP

BUG'S ACTIONS:

PHOTO/DRAWING

NOTES:

BUG IDENTIFICATION LOG

DATE: | TIME: | SEASON:

LOCATION:

BUG NAME:

BUG COLORS:

NUMBER OF LEGS: | DOES IT HAVE WINGS: ☐ YES ☐ NO ☐ NOT SURE

BUG DESCRIPTION:

DOES IT MAKE ANY SOUNDS? ☐ YES ☐ NO | WAS IT ALONE OR IN A GROUP? ☐ ALONE ☐ GROUP

BUG'S ACTIONS:

PHOTO/DRAWING

NOTES:

BUG IDENTIFICATION LOG

DATE:	TIME:	SEASON:

LOCATION:

BUG NAME:

BUG COLORS:

NUMBER OF LEGS:	DOES IT HAVE WINGS: ☐ YES ☐ NO ☐ NOT SURE

BUG DESCRIPTION:

DOES IT MAKE ANY SOUNDS? ☐ YES ☐ NO	WAS IT ALONE OR IN A GROUP? ☐ ALONE ☐ GROUP

BUG'S ACTIONS:

PHOTO/DRAWING

NOTES:

BUG IDENTIFICATION LOG

DATE:	TIME:	SEASON:

LOCATION:

BUG NAME:

BUG COLORS:

NUMBER OF LEGS:	DOES IT HAVE WINGS: ☐ YES ☐ NO ☐ NOT SURE

BUG DESCRIPTION:

DOES IT MAKE ANY SOUNDS? ☐ YES ☐ NO	WAS IT ALONE OR IN A GROUP? ☐ ALONE ☐ GROUP

BUG'S ACTIONS:

PHOTO/DRAWING

NOTES:

BUG IDENTIFICATION LOG

DATE: | TIME: | SEASON:

LOCATION:

BUG NAME:

BUG COLORS:

NUMBER OF LEGS: | DOES IT HAVE WINGS: ☐ YES ☐ NO ☐ NOT SURE

BUG DESCRIPTION:

DOES IT MAKE ANY SOUNDS? ☐ YES ☐ NO | WAS IT ALONE OR IN A GROUP? ☐ ALONE ☐ GROUP

BUG'S ACTIONS:

PHOTO/DRAWING

NOTES:

BUG IDENTIFICATION LOG

DATE:	TIME:	SEASON:

LOCATION:

BUG NAME:

BUG COLORS:

NUMBER OF LEGS:	DOES IT HAVE WINGS: ☐ YES ☐ NO ☐ NOT SURE

BUG DESCRIPTION:

DOES IT MAKE ANY SOUNDS? ☐ YES ☐ NO	WAS IT ALONE OR IN A GROUP? ☐ ALONE ☐ GROUP

BUG'S ACTIONS:

PHOTO/DRAWING

NOTES:

BUG IDENTIFICATION LOG

DATE: | TIME: | SEASON:

LOCATION:

BUG NAME:

BUG COLORS:

NUMBER OF LEGS: | DOES IT HAVE WINGS: ☐ YES ☐ NO ☐ NOT SURE

BUG DESCRIPTION:

DOES IT MAKE ANY SOUNDS? ☐ YES ☐ NO | WAS IT ALONE OR IN A GROUP? ☐ ALONE ☐ GROUP

BUG'S ACTIONS:

PHOTO/DRAWING

NOTES:

BUG IDENTIFICATION LOG

DATE:	TIME:	SEASON:

LOCATION:

BUG NAME:

BUG COLORS:

NUMBER OF LEGS:	DOES IT HAVE WINGS: ☐ YES ☐ NO ☐ NOT SURE

BUG DESCRIPTION:

DOES IT MAKE ANY SOUNDS? ☐ YES ☐ NO	WAS IT ALONE OR IN A GROUP? ☐ ALONE ☐ GROUP

BUG'S ACTIONS:

PHOTO/DRAWING

NOTES:

BUG IDENTIFICATION LOG

DATE: | TIME: | SEASON:

LOCATION:

BUG NAME:

BUG COLORS:

NUMBER OF LEGS: | DOES IT HAVE WINGS: ☐ YES ☐ NO ☐ NOT SURE

BUG DESCRIPTION:

DOES IT MAKE ANY SOUNDS? ☐ YES ☐ NO | WAS IT ALONE OR IN A GROUP? ☐ ALONE ☐ GROUP

BUG'S ACTIONS:

PHOTO/DRAWING

NOTES:

BUG IDENTIFICATION LOG

DATE: | TIME: | SEASON:

LOCATION:

BUG NAME:

BUG COLORS:

NUMBER OF LEGS: | DOES IT HAVE WINGS: ☐ YES ☐ NO ☐ NOT SURE

BUG DESCRIPTION:

DOES IT MAKE ANY SOUNDS? ☐ YES ☐ NO | WAS IT ALONE OR IN A GROUP? ☐ ALONE ☐ GROUP

BUG'S ACTIONS:

PHOTO/DRAWING

NOTES:

BUG IDENTIFICATION LOG

DATE: | TIME: | SEASON:

LOCATION:

BUG NAME:

BUG COLORS:

NUMBER OF LEGS: | DOES IT HAVE WINGS: ☐ YES ☐ NO ☐ NOT SURE

BUG DESCRIPTION:

DOES IT MAKE ANY SOUNDS? ☐ YES ☐ NO | WAS IT ALONE OR IN A GROUP? ☐ ALONE ☐ GROUP

BUG'S ACTIONS:

PHOTO/DRAWING

NOTES:

BUG IDENTIFICATION LOG

DATE: | TIME: | SEASON:

LOCATION:

BUG NAME:

BUG COLORS:

NUMBER OF LEGS: | DOES IT HAVE WINGS: ☐ YES ☐ NO ☐ NOT SURE

BUG DESCRIPTION:

DOES IT MAKE ANY SOUNDS? ☐ YES ☐ NO | WAS IT ALONE OR IN A GROUP? ☐ ALONE ☐ GROUP

BUG'S ACTIONS:

PHOTO/DRAWING

NOTES:

BUG IDENTIFICATION LOG

DATE:	TIME:	SEASON:

LOCATION:

BUG NAME:

BUG COLORS:

NUMBER OF LEGS:	DOES IT HAVE WINGS: ☐ YES ☐ NO ☐ NOT SURE

BUG DESCRIPTION:

DOES IT MAKE ANY SOUNDS? ☐ YES ☐ NO	WAS IT ALONE OR IN A GROUP? ☐ ALONE ☐ GROUP

BUG'S ACTIONS:

PHOTO/DRAWING

NOTES:

BUG IDENTIFICATION LOG

DATE:	TIME:	SEASON:

LOCATION:

BUG NAME:

BUG COLORS:

NUMBER OF LEGS:	DOES IT HAVE WINGS:	☐ YES	☐ NO	☐ NOT SURE

BUG DESCRIPTION:

DOES IT MAKE ANY SOUNDS? ☐ YES ☐ NO	WAS IT ALONE OR IN A GROUP? ☐ ALONE ☐ GROUP

BUG'S ACTIONS:

PHOTO/DRAWING

NOTES:

BUG I-E TIFICATIO LOG

DATE: | TIME: | SEASON:

LOCATION:

BUG NAME:

BUG COLORS:

NUMBER OF LEGS: | DOES IT HAVE WINGS: ☐ YES ☐ NO ☐ NOT SURE

BUG DESCRIPTION:

DOES IT MAKE ANY SOUNDS? ☐ YES ☐ NO | WAS IT ALONE OR IN A GROUP? ☐ ALONE ☐ GROUP

BUG'S ACTIONS:

PHOTO/DRAWING

NOTES:

BUG IDENTIFICATION LOG

DATE:	TIME:	SEASON:

LOCATION:

BUG NAME:

BUG COLORS:

NUMBER OF LEGS:	DOES IT HAVE WINGS: ☐ YES ☐ NO ☐ NOT SURE

BUG DESCRIPTION:

DOES IT MAKE ANY SOUNDS? ☐ YES ☐ NO	WAS IT ALONE OR IN A GROUP? ☐ ALONE ☐ GROUP

BUG'S ACTIONS:

PHOTO/DRAWING

NOTES:

BUG IDENTIFICATION LOG

DATE:	TIME:	SEASON:

LOCATION:

BUG NAME:

BUG COLORS:

NUMBER OF LEGS:	DOES IT HAVE WINGS: ☐ YES ☐ NO ☐ NOT SURE

BUG DESCRIPTION:

DOES IT MAKE ANY SOUNDS? ☐ YES ☐ NO	WAS IT ALONE OR IN A GROUP? ☐ ALONE ☐ GROUP

BUG'S ACTIONS:

PHOTO/DRAWING

NOTES:

BUG IDENTIFICATION LOG

DATE:	TIME:	SEASON:

LOCATION:

BUG NAME:

BUG COLORS:

NUMBER OF LEGS:	DOES IT HAVE WINGS: ☐ YES ☐ NO ☐ NOT SURE

BUG DESCRIPTION:

DOES IT MAKE ANY SOUNDS? ☐ YES ☐ NO	WAS IT ALONE OR IN A GROUP? ☐ ALONE ☐ GROUP

BUG'S ACTIONS:

PHOTO/DRAWING

NOTES:

BUG IDENTIFICATION LOG

DATE:	TIME:	SEASON:

LOCATION:

BUG NAME:

BUG COLORS:

NUMBER OF LEGS:	DOES IT HAVE WINGS: ☐ YES ☐ NO ☐ NOT SURE

BUG DESCRIPTION:

DOES IT MAKE ANY SOUNDS? ☐ YES ☐ NO	WAS IT ALONE OR IN A GROUP? ☐ ALONE ☐ GROUP

BUG'S ACTIONS:

PHOTO/DRAWING

NOTES:

BUG IDENTIFICATION LOG

DATE:	TIME:	SEASON:

LOCATION:

BUG NAME:

BUG COLORS:

NUMBER OF LEGS:	DOES IT HAVE WINGS: ☐ YES ☐ NO ☐ NOT SURE

BUG DESCRIPTION:

DOES IT MAKE ANY SOUNDS? ☐ YES ☐ NO	WAS IT ALONE OR IN A GROUP? ☐ ALONE ☐ GROUP

BUG'S ACTIONS:

PHOTO/DRAWING

NOTES:

BUG IDENTIFICATION LOG

DATE: | TIME: | SEASON:

LOCATION:

BUG NAME:

BUG COLORS:

NUMBER OF LEGS: | DOES IT HAVE WINGS: ☐ YES ☐ NO ☐ NOT SURE

BUG DESCRIPTION:

DOES IT MAKE ANY SOUNDS? ☐ YES ☐ NO | WAS IT ALONE OR IN A GROUP? ☐ ALONE ☐ GROUP

BUG'S ACTIONS:

PHOTO/DRAWING

NOTES:

BUG IDENTIFICATION LOG

DATE:	TIME:	SEASON:

LOCATION:

BUG NAME:

BUG COLORS:

NUMBER OF LEGS:	DOES IT HAVE WINGS: ☐ YES ☐ NO ☐ NOT SURE

BUG DESCRIPTION:

DOES IT MAKE ANY SOUNDS? ☐ YES ☐ NO	WAS IT ALONE OR IN A GROUP? ☐ ALONE ☐ GROUP

BUG'S ACTIONS:

PHOTO/DRAWING

NOTES:

BUG IDENTIFICATION LOG

DATE: | TIME: | SEASON:

LOCATION:

BUG NAME:

BUG COLORS:

NUMBER OF LEGS: | DOES IT HAVE WINGS: ☐ YES ☐ NO ☐ NOT SURE

BUG DESCRIPTION:

DOES IT MAKE ANY SOUNDS? ☐ YES ☐ NO | WAS IT ALONE OR IN A GROUP? ☐ ALONE ☐ GROUP

BUG'S ACTIONS:

PHOTO/DRAWING

NOTES:

BUG IDENTIFICATION LOG

DATE:	TIME:	SEASON:

LOCATION:

BUG NAME:

BUG COLORS:

NUMBER OF LEGS:	DOES IT HAVE WINGS: ☐ YES ☐ NO ☐ NOT SURE

BUG DESCRIPTION:

DOES IT MAKE ANY SOUNDS? ☐ YES ☐ NO	WAS IT ALONE OR IN A GROUP? ☐ ALONE ☐ GROUP

BUG'S ACTIONS:

PHOTO/DRAWING

NOTES:

BUG IDENTIFICATION LOG

DATE:	TIME:	SEASON:

LOCATION:

BUG NAME:

BUG COLORS:

NUMBER OF LEGS:	DOES IT HAVE WINGS: ☐ YES ☐ NO ☐ NOT SURE

BUG DESCRIPTION:

DOES IT MAKE ANY SOUNDS? ☐ YES ☐ NO	WAS IT ALONE OR IN A GROUP? ☐ ALONE ☐ GROUP

BUG'S ACTIONS:

PHOTO/DRAWING

NOTES:

BUG IDENTIFICATION LOG

DATE:	TIME:	SEASON:

LOCATION:

BUG NAME:

BUG COLORS:

NUMBER OF LEGS:	DOES IT HAVE WINGS:	☐ YES	☐ NO	☐ NOT SURE

BUG DESCRIPTION:

DOES IT MAKE ANY SOUNDS? ☐ YES ☐ NO	WAS IT ALONE OR IN A GROUP? ☐ ALONE ☐ GROUP

BUG'S ACTIONS:

PHOTO/DRAWING

NOTES:

BUG IDENTIFICATION LOG

DATE: | TIME: | SEASON:

LOCATION:

BUG NAME:

BUG COLORS:

NUMBER OF LEGS: | DOES IT HAVE WINGS: ☐ YES ☐ NO ☐ NOT SURE

BUG DESCRIPTION:

DOES IT MAKE ANY SOUNDS? ☐ YES ☐ NO | WAS IT ALONE OR IN A GROUP? ☐ ALONE ☐ GROUP

BUG'S ACTIONS:

PHOTO/DRAWING

NOTES:

BUG IDENTIFICATION LOG

DATE:	TIME:	SEASON:

LOCATION:

BUG NAME:

BUG COLORS:

NUMBER OF LEGS:	DOES IT HAVE WINGS: ☐ YES ☐ NO ☐ NOT SURE

BUG DESCRIPTION:

DOES IT MAKE ANY SOUNDS? ☐ YES ☐ NO	WAS IT ALONE OR IN A GROUP? ☐ ALONE ☐ GROUP

BUG'S ACTIONS:

PHOTO/DRAWING

NOTES:

BUG IDENTIFICATION LOG

DATE:	TIME:	SEASON:

LOCATION:

BUG NAME:

BUG COLORS:

NUMBER OF LEGS:	DOES IT HAVE WINGS: ☐ YES ☐ NO ☐ NOT SURE

BUG DESCRIPTION:

DOES IT MAKE ANY SOUNDS? ☐ YES ☐ NO	WAS IT ALONE OR IN A GROUP? ☐ ALONE ☐ GROUP

BUG'S ACTIONS:

PHOTO/DRAWING

NOTES:

BUG IDENTIFICATION LOG

DATE:	TIME:	SEASON:

LOCATION:

BUG NAME:

BUG COLORS:

NUMBER OF LEGS:	DOES IT HAVE WINGS: ☐ YES ☐ NO ☐ NOT SURE

BUG DESCRIPTION:

DOES IT MAKE ANY SOUNDS? ☐ YES ☐ NO	WAS IT ALONE OR IN A GROUP? ☐ ALONE ☐ GROUP

BUG'S ACTIONS:

PHOTO/DRAWING

NOTES:

BUG IDENTIFICATION LOG

DATE: | TIME: | SEASON:

LOCATION:

BUG NAME:

BUG COLORS:

NUMBER OF LEGS: | DOES IT HAVE WINGS: ☐ YES ☐ NO ☐ NOT SURE

BUG DESCRIPTION:

DOES IT MAKE ANY SOUNDS? ☐ YES ☐ NO | WAS IT ALONE OR IN A GROUP? ☐ ALONE ☐ GROUP

BUG'S ACTIONS:

PHOTO/DRAWING

NOTES:

BUG IDENTIFICATION LOG

DATE:	TIME:	SEASON:

LOCATION:

BUG NAME:

BUG COLORS:

NUMBER OF LEGS:	DOES IT HAVE WINGS: ☐ YES ☐ NO ☐ NOT SURE

BUG DESCRIPTION:

DOES IT MAKE ANY SOUNDS? ☐ YES ☐ NO	WAS IT ALONE OR IN A GROUP? ☐ ALONE ☐ GROUP

BUG'S ACTIONS:

PHOTO/DRAWING

NOTES:

BUG IDENTIFICATION LOG

DATE:	TIME:	SEASON:

LOCATION:

BUG NAME:

BUG COLORS:

NUMBER OF LEGS:	DOES IT HAVE WINGS: ☐ YES ☐ NO ☐ NOT SURE

BUG DESCRIPTION:

DOES IT MAKE ANY SOUNDS? ☐ YES ☐ NO	WAS IT ALONE OR IN A GROUP? ☐ ALONE ☐ GROUP

BUG'S ACTIONS:

PHOTO/DRAWING

NOTES:

BUG IDENTIFICATION LOG

DATE:	TIME:	SEASON:

LOCATION:

BUG NAME:

BUG COLORS:

NUMBER OF LEGS:	DOES IT HAVE WINGS: ☐ YES ☐ NO ☐ NOT SURE

BUG DESCRIPTION:

DOES IT MAKE ANY SOUNDS? ☐ YES ☐ NO	WAS IT ALONE OR IN A GROUP? ☐ ALONE ☐ GROUP

BUG'S ACTIONS:

PHOTO/DRAWING

NOTES:

BUG IDENTIFICATION LOG

DATE:	TIME:	SEASON:

LOCATION:

BUG NAME:

BUG COLORS:

NUMBER OF LEGS:	DOES IT HAVE WINGS: ☐ YES ☐ NO ☐ NOT SURE

BUG DESCRIPTION:

DOES IT MAKE ANY SOUNDS? ☐ YES ☐ NO	WAS IT ALONE OR IN A GROUP? ☐ ALONE ☐ GROUP

BUG'S ACTIONS:

PHOTO/DRAWING

NOTES:

BUG IDENTIFICATION LOG

DATE: | TIME: | SEASON:

LOCATION:

BUG NAME:

BUG COLORS:

NUMBER OF LEGS: | DOES IT HAVE WINGS: ☐ YES ☐ NO ☐ NOT SURE

BUG DESCRIPTION:

DOES IT MAKE ANY SOUNDS? ☐ YES ☐ NO | WAS IT ALONE OR IN A GROUP? ☐ ALONE ☐ GROUP

BUG'S ACTIONS:

PHOTO/DRAWING

NOTES:

BUG IDENTIFICATION LOG

DATE:	TIME:	SEASON:

LOCATION:

BUG NAME:

BUG COLORS:

NUMBER OF LEGS:	DOES IT HAVE WINGS: ☐ YES ☐ NO ☐ NOT SURE

BUG DESCRIPTION:

DOES IT MAKE ANY SOUNDS? ☐ YES ☐ NO	WAS IT ALONE OR IN A GROUP? ☐ ALONE ☐ GROUP

BUG'S ACTIONS:

PHOTO/DRAWING

NOTES:

BUG IDENTIFICATION LOG

DATE:	TIME:	SEASON:

LOCATION:

BUG NAME:

BUG COLORS:

NUMBER OF LEGS:	DOES IT HAVE WINGS: ☐ YES ☐ NO ☐ NOT SURE

BUG DESCRIPTION:

DOES IT MAKE ANY SOUNDS? ☐ YES ☐ NO	WAS IT ALONE OR IN A GROUP? ☐ ALONE ☐ GROUP

BUG'S ACTIONS:

PHOTO/DRAWING

NOTES:

BUG IDENTIFICATION LOG

DATE:	TIME:	SEASON:

LOCATION:

BUG NAME:

BUG COLORS:

NUMBER OF LEGS:	DOES IT HAVE WINGS: ☐ YES ☐ NO ☐ NOT SURE

BUG DESCRIPTION:

DOES IT MAKE ANY SOUNDS? ☐ YES ☐ NO	WAS IT ALONE OR IN A GROUP? ☐ ALONE ☐ GROUP

BUG'S ACTIONS:

PHOTO/DRAWING

NOTES:

BUG IDENTIFICATION LOG

DATE:	TIME:	SEASON:

LOCATION:

BUG NAME:

BUG COLORS:

NUMBER OF LEGS:	DOES IT HAVE WINGS: ☐ YES ☐ NO ☐ NOT SURE

BUG DESCRIPTION:

DOES IT MAKE ANY SOUNDS? ☐ YES ☐ NO	WAS IT ALONE OR IN A GROUP? ☐ ALONE ☐ GROUP

BUG'S ACTIONS:

PHOTO/DRAWING

NOTES:

BUG IDENTIFICATION LOG

DATE:	TIME:	SEASON:

LOCATION:

BUG NAME:

BUG COLORS:

NUMBER OF LEGS:	DOES IT HAVE WINGS: ☐ YES ☐ NO ☐ NOT SURE

BUG DESCRIPTION:

DOES IT MAKE ANY SOUNDS? ☐ YES ☐ NO	WAS IT ALONE OR IN A GROUP? ☐ ALONE ☐ GROUP

BUG'S ACTIONS:

PHOTO/DRAWING

NOTES:

BUG IDENTIFICATION LOG

DATE:	TIME:	SEASON:

LOCATION:

BUG NAME:

BUG COLORS:

NUMBER OF LEGS:	DOES IT HAVE WINGS: ☐ YES ☐ NO ☐ NOT SURE

BUG DESCRIPTION:

DOES IT MAKE ANY SOUNDS? ☐ YES ☐ NO	WAS IT ALONE OR IN A GROUP? ☐ ALONE ☐ GROUP

BUG'S ACTIONS:

PHOTO/DRAWING

NOTES:

BUG IDENTIFICATION LOG

DATE:	TIME:	SEASON:

LOCATION:

BUG NAME:

BUG COLORS:

NUMBER OF LEGS:	DOES IT HAVE WINGS: ☐ YES ☐ NO ☐ NOT SURE

BUG DESCRIPTION:

DOES IT MAKE ANY SOUNDS? ☐ YES ☐ NO	WAS IT ALONE OR IN A GROUP? ☐ ALONE ☐ GROUP

BUG'S ACTIONS:

PHOTO/DRAWING

NOTES:

BUG IDENTIFICATION LOG

DATE:	TIME:	SEASON:

LOCATION:

BUG NAME:

BUG COLORS:

NUMBER OF LEGS:	DOES IT HAVE WINGS: ☐ YES ☐ NO ☐ NOT SURE

BUG DESCRIPTION:

DOES IT MAKE ANY SOUNDS? ☐ YES ☐ NO	WAS IT ALONE OR IN A GROUP? ☐ ALONE ☐ GROUP

BUG'S ACTIONS:

PHOTO/DRAWING

NOTES:

BUG IDENTIFICATION LOG

DATE:	TIME:	SEASON:

LOCATION:

BUG NAME:

BUG COLORS:

NUMBER OF LEGS:	DOES IT HAVE WINGS: ☐ YES ☐ NO ☐ NOT SURE

BUG DESCRIPTION:

DOES IT MAKE ANY SOUNDS? ☐ YES ☐ NO	WAS IT ALONE OR IN A GROUP? ☐ ALONE ☐ GROUP

BUG'S ACTIONS:

PHOTO/DRAWING

NOTES:

BUG IDENTIFICATION LOG

DATE:	TIME:	SEASON:

LOCATION:

BUG NAME:

BUG COLORS:

NUMBER OF LEGS:	DOES IT HAVE WINGS: ☐ YES ☐ NO ☐ NOT SURE

BUG DESCRIPTION:

DOES IT MAKE ANY SOUNDS? ☐ YES ☐ NO	WAS IT ALONE OR IN A GROUP? ☐ ALONE ☐ GROUP

BUG'S ACTIONS:

PHOTO/DRAWING

NOTES:

BUG IDENTIFICATION LOG

DATE: | TIME: | SEASON:

LOCATION:

BUG NAME:

BUG COLORS:

NUMBER OF LEGS: | DOES IT HAVE WINGS: ☐ YES ☐ NO ☐ NOT SURE

BUG DESCRIPTION:

DOES IT MAKE ANY SOUNDS? ☐ YES ☐ NO | WAS IT ALONE OR IN A GROUP? ☐ ALONE ☐ GROUP

BUG'S ACTIONS:

PHOTO/DRAWING

NOTES:

BUG IDENTIFICATION LOG

DATE:	TIME:	SEASON:

LOCATION:

BUG NAME:

BUG COLORS:

NUMBER OF LEGS:	DOES IT HAVE WINGS: ☐ YES ☐ NO ☐ NOT SURE

BUG DESCRIPTION:

DOES IT MAKE ANY SOUNDS? ☐ YES ☐ NO	WAS IT ALONE OR IN A GROUP? ☐ ALONE ☐ GROUP

BUG'S ACTIONS:

PHOTO/DRAWING

NOTES:

BUG IDENTIFICATION LOG

DATE: | TIME: | SEASON:

LOCATION:

BUG NAME:

BUG COLORS:

NUMBER OF LEGS: | DOES IT HAVE WINGS: ☐ YES ☐ NO ☐ NOT SURE

BUG DESCRIPTION:

DOES IT MAKE ANY SOUNDS? ☐ YES ☐ NO | WAS IT ALONE OR IN A GROUP? ☐ ALONE ☐ GROUP

BUG'S ACTIONS:

PHOTO/DRAWING

NOTES:

BUG IDENTIFICATION LOG

DATE:	TIME:	SEASON:

LOCATION:

BUG NAME:

BUG COLORS:

NUMBER OF LEGS:	DOES IT HAVE WINGS: ☐ YES ☐ NO ☐ NOT SURE

BUG DESCRIPTION:

DOES IT MAKE ANY SOUNDS? ☐ YES ☐ NO	WAS IT ALONE OR IN A GROUP? ☐ ALONE ☐ GROUP

BUG'S ACTIONS:

PHOTO/DRAWING

NOTES:

BUG IDENTIFICATION LOG

DATE:	TIME:	SEASON:

LOCATION:

BUG NAME:

BUG COLORS:

NUMBER OF LEGS:	DOES IT HAVE WINGS: ☐ YES ☐ NO ☐ NOT SURE

BUG DESCRIPTION:

DOES IT MAKE ANY SOUNDS? ☐ YES ☐ NO	WAS IT ALONE OR IN A GROUP? ☐ ALONE ☐ GROUP

BUG'S ACTIONS:

PHOTO/DRAWING

NOTES:

BUG IDENTIFICATION LOG

DATE:	TIME:	SEASON:

LOCATION:

BUG NAME:

BUG COLORS:

NUMBER OF LEGS:	DOES IT HAVE WINGS: ☐ YES ☐ NO ☐ NOT SURE

BUG DESCRIPTION:

DOES IT MAKE ANY SOUNDS? ☐ YES ☐ NO	WAS IT ALONE OR IN A GROUP? ☐ ALONE ☐ GROUP

BUG'S ACTIONS:

PHOTO/DRAWING

NOTES:

BUG IDENTIFICATION LOG

DATE:	TIME:	SEASON:

LOCATION:

BUG NAME:

BUG COLORS:

NUMBER OF LEGS:	DOES IT HAVE WINGS: ☐ YES ☐ NO ☐ NOT SURE

BUG DESCRIPTION:

DOES IT MAKE ANY SOUNDS? ☐ YES ☐ NO	WAS IT ALONE OR IN A GROUP? ☐ ALONE ☐ GROUP

BUG'S ACTIONS:

PHOTO/DRAWING

NOTES:

BUG IDENTIFICATION LOG

DATE:	TIME:	SEASON:

LOCATION:

BUG NAME:

BUG COLORS:

NUMBER OF LEGS:	DOES IT HAVE WINGS: ☐ YES ☐ NO ☐ NOT SURE

BUG DESCRIPTION:

DOES IT MAKE ANY SOUNDS? ☐ YES ☐ NO	WAS IT ALONE OR IN A GROUP? ☐ ALONE ☐ GROUP

BUG'S ACTIONS:

PHOTO/DRAWING

NOTES:

BUG IDENTIFICATION LOG

DATE: | TIME: | SEASON:

LOCATION:

BUG NAME:

BUG COLORS:

NUMBER OF LEGS: | DOES IT HAVE WINGS: ☐ YES ☐ NO ☐ NOT SURE

BUG DESCRIPTION:

DOES IT MAKE ANY SOUNDS? ☐ YES ☐ NO | WAS IT ALONE OR IN A GROUP? ☐ ALONE ☐ GROUP

BUG'S ACTIONS:

PHOTO/DRAWING

NOTES:

BUG IDENTIFICATION LOG

DATE:	TIME:	SEASON:

LOCATION:

BUG NAME:

BUG COLORS:

NUMBER OF LEGS:	DOES IT HAVE WINGS: ☐ YES ☐ NO ☐ NOT SURE

BUG DESCRIPTION:

DOES IT MAKE ANY SOUNDS? ☐ YES ☐ NO	WAS IT ALONE OR IN A GROUP? ☐ ALONE ☐ GROUP

BUG'S ACTIONS:

PHOTO/DRAWING

NOTES:

BUG IDENTIFICATION LOG

DATE:	TIME:	SEASON:

LOCATION:

BUG NAME:

BUG COLORS:

NUMBER OF LEGS:	DOES IT HAVE WINGS: ☐ YES ☐ NO ☐ NOT SURE

BUG DESCRIPTION:

DOES IT MAKE ANY SOUNDS? ☐ YES ☐ NO	WAS IT ALONE OR IN A GROUP? ☐ ALONE ☐ GROUP

BUG'S ACTIONS:

PHOTO/DRAWING

NOTES:

BUG IDENTIFICATION LOG

DATE:	TIME:	SEASON:

LOCATION:

BUG NAME:

BUG COLORS:

NUMBER OF LEGS:	DOES IT HAVE WINGS:	☐ YES	☐ NO	☐ NOT SURE

BUG DESCRIPTION:

DOES IT MAKE ANY SOUNDS? ☐ YES ☐ NO | WAS IT ALONE OR IN A GROUP? ☐ ALONE ☐ GROUP

BUG'S ACTIONS:

PHOTO/DRAWING

NOTES:

BUG IDENTIFICATION LOG

DATE:	TIME:	SEASON:

LOCATION:

BUG NAME:

BUG COLORS:

NUMBER OF LEGS:	DOES IT HAVE WINGS: ☐ YES ☐ NO ☐ NOT SURE

BUG DESCRIPTION:

DOES IT MAKE ANY SOUNDS? ☐ YES ☐ NO	WAS IT ALONE OR IN A GROUP? ☐ ALONE ☐ GROUP

BUG'S ACTIONS:

PHOTO/DRAWING

NOTES:

Made in the USA
Middletown, DE
05 April 2023

28300949R00068